Fossils on a Red Flag

poems by

Amelia Díaz Ettinger

Finishing Line Press
Georgetown, Kentucky

Fossils on a Red Flag

James, Thank you
so much for the faith
you have given me, and
all your encouragement —

Lots of Love,

Amelia Díaz Ettinger

ACKNOWLEDGMENTS

Gracias:
I would like to thank the Grande Ronde and Blue Mountain poets who have
shared their ideas about this work, particularly James Benson for his reading
of this manuscript.

Publisher: Leah Huete de Maines
Editor: Christen Kincaid
Author Photo: April Van Tassell
Cover Art and Design: Kristin Summers @ Redbat Design

Printed in the USA on acid-free paper.
Order online: www.finishinglinepress.com
           also available on amazon.com

Author inquiries and mail orders:
Finishing Line Press
P. O. Box 1626
Georgetown, Kentucky 40324
U. S. A.

Table of Contents

To the people of Culebra and
to Susan Dinga.

Executive Order 8684

EXECUTIVE ORDER

———

ESTABLISHING CULEBRA ISLAND NAVAL DEFENSIVE SEA
AREA AND CULEBRA ISLAND NAVAL AIRSPACE RESERVATION

PUERTO RICO

By virtue of the authority vested in me by the provisions of section 44 of the Criminal Code, as amended
(U.S.C., title 18, sec. 96), and section 4 of the Air
Commerce Act approved May 20, 1926 (44 Stat. 570, U.S.C.,
title 49, sec. 174), the territorial waters between the
extreme high-water mark and the three-mile marine boun-
dary surrounding the island of Culebra, Puerto Rico, are
hereby established and reserved as a naval defensive sea
area for purposes of national defense, such area to be
known as "Culebra Island Naval Defensive Sea Area"; and
the airspace over the said territorial waters and island is hereby set apart and reserved as a naval airspace reservation for purposes of national defense, such
reservation to be known as "Culebra Island Naval Airspace
Reservation".

At no time shall any person, other than persons on
public vessels of the United States, enter Culebra Island
Naval Defensive Sea Area, nor shall any vessel or other
craft, other than public vessels of the United States, be
navigated into said area, unless authorized by the Secretary of the Navy.

At no time shall any aircraft, other than public aircraft of the United States, be navigated into Culebra Island Naval Airspace Reservation, unless authorized by the Secretary of the Navy.

The provisions of the preceding paragraphs shall be enforced by the Secretary of the Navy, with the cooperation of the local law enforcement officers of the United States and of the Government of Puerto Rico, and the Secretary of the Navy is hereby authorized to prescribe such regulations as may be necessary to carry out such provisions.

Any person violating any of the provisions of this order relating to Culebra Island Naval Defensive Sea Area shall be subject to the penalties provided by section 44 of the Criminal Code as amended (U.S.C., title 18, sec. 96), and any person violating any of the provisions of this order relating to Culebra Island Naval Airspace Reservation shall be subject to the penalties prescribed by the Civil Aeronautics Act of 1938 (52 Stat. 973).

This order shall take effect ninety days after date hereof.

Franklin D Roosevelt

The White House,
February 14, 1941.

8684

xii

1941* half life: EO 8684

Our sons had been fighting that war
wedged in an unimaginable cold land,
      —if not for the radio at the tavern.
Too distant from these warm shores,
      waters that could not touch each other
you knew and stood proudly
           —the 65th Infantry
even when they came back in boxes.
And yet, we were prohibited
      1.   to swim
      2.   fish
      3.   leave
      4.   or enter
the island we always called home,
Culebra
since the times of Agüeybaná.

I am a child again today,
with a different captain at the helm.
      —The crown defeated is a distant memory
An infant citizen
without protection
nor benediction.
Our lips sewn shut
you don't dare to look at what you see
your eyes have been moved inside your throat
your lips open only to this list
seek permission from your new father,
the Admiral,
he might then grant you
a permission to breathe
          as long as you don't find your voice.

1946* half life

They thought themselves safe,
under their pedigree of fifty stars,
six officers and three enlisted men.
On that day in May,
were they listening to *Mi Mulata*,
or *White Christmas*?
Maybe they had a royal flush,
savoring the northern Bacardi
or the southern Don Q with drops
of coconut water, or even better, mango.
Certainly, they were drinking
the vastness of pink and white sand
against a green sea, el Caribe bello.
Some might have envisioned
a truncated conversation,
"Let me show you," they would have started,
"the bay with its own pale light,
that owns the stars at night,
the breeze that tastes of seafood."
But the observation post with its hammocks
and the target were painted gray,
and seagulls and roseate turns flew
screaming their alarms
as the dust dispersed reddening
the incoming night.

The wives and mothers on the other side
of that ocean don't believe words
like friendly fire.

Public Statement:
April 24, 1970

"This part of the island has been used continuously since 1936 for ships' gunfire practice, and during that long period of time no one has been killed or injured as a result of this training."

Admiral Matter

So, the stars were blinded from both sides,
the convenience of selective

blindness.

1968*half life

The birds thought themselves safe.
No barbwires in the open air.
No red flags to shame their passage.
They were safe, a home in the Caribbean,
a national wildlife refuge,
the first in the archipelago. [1909]
They came for the pleasure of white
and pink sands, and turquoise waters abundant.
Diving into those waters,
dropping like bombs from the sky,
you could hear their pleasure
in their straight narrow dives.
Twin Rocks harbored their nests.
This sea heralds the arrival
of the next generation
their jocular conglomerations
muted the sound of waves.
A visible camaraderie.
They were parents here, and aunts
and siblings.
They knew and fed each other's chicks.
　　—Safe—
a mighty small word
when all their white and black feathers darkened the sky
just seconds, while thousand
of sooty turns bathed
on a sea of rust.
The inferno that followed
charred the anxious waiting families
sitting peacefully at their nests.

Senator Goodel expresses concern, "the impact area an ecological disaster...the number that were destroyed is enormous."

Queen Conch I

I knew birds and turtles,
and where each spawned
the next generation.
So, in cut-off jeans,
that showed
the tender moons
of my upper thighs,
I went, telescope and binoculars at hand, to a refuge,
with no knowledge of its past nor
the sledgehammer present, I was trespassing.
I had not heard of the red flag at the hilltop,
or post office directives,
or of a Navy,
or the taking of Culebra in 1906.
Again, wrapped in loud youth, unaware
of the tree ducks' eyes that followed
my unconscious march.
A discarded paper flew
"Culebra para los Culebrenses."

I swam

Queen Conch II

Strombus gigas, to be sure, so named by Linnaeus in 1758
a shell like no other with hard points and convolutions.
An ocean rests inside its marbled walls,
Children make lamps to sell to tourists.
But they were revered by los hombres de Culebra
fishing at Luis Peña Cay.

After a day at sea, with black nets filled
with thousands of silver and red struggling gills,
those fluted conchs alert those
who waited patiently at Dewey Bay.
The call that filled the air with abundance
and alerted the roseate tern, la palometa
to dip close to the nets and stab.

Queen Conch III

I met a woman, Susan,
her voice that tasted of ocean
      alerted me
            —You are not free
            to walk, to be
            wait,
            no red flag
            we swim.
So, I looked away from her eyes
and her long blonde hair,
the sky was clear, I pointed
'A magnificent *Tijereta*'.
Missiles at close range still unknown.
The land that day did not tremble
Two green turtles laid eggs
sand made their eyes cry.

Queen Conch IV

A bed of turtlegrass gave us dinner.
Strombus gigas, the queen conch
large fluted lip a gash in pink
like the opening between the woman's legs

She showed me how to pull the meat
I show her the radula and my ignorance,
how could I know then
the pain of a young mother?

> Her son awoke at night
> to sound of rockets
> and grenades
> hiding near his crib.

The foot of the mollusk looked like a man's tongue.
With a wooden pilón she pounded the flesh
flat so it could no longer talk
Fried it in garlic and flour
until no cell was left alive.

*1970 half life   *"I have my orders.*

We will blow up some
more on Monday."

Thirty-five years of missiles
accumulated around the protective growth of polyps.
Sea anemones, and ocean feathers decorated some
while the yellow grunts, blue palometas, and multicolored jodes
swam in swarms to feed generations.
Jellyfish lazily floated
and moray eels dashed
along with the tepid currents.

Coronel Bennett instructed, and the frogmen
stacked shell by undetonated shell on top of this reef,
not in the distant depths of the sandy ocean, miles from life.
Their metal casting crushing the weight of a thousand years of polyp
growth.
A pin was pulled,
a second for all those years to evaporate.

Two hundred feet from the explosion
the coral was sliced as by a divine indifferent knife,
white spots already spread, where life had been blasted.
The shore filled with the glassy eyes of fish
and the thunderstruck expression of the Culebran fishermen
who saw in that carpet of silent gills and guts the dawn of their
starvation.

Claro Feliciano, a citizen of Culebra
age 74 in 1970*half life

The Navy was a ghost for him,
     "La Marina es un fantasma."
He could taste and feel its grip.
He foretold the phantom
would take his last meal.
From an ocean diseased with radiation.
     "Ese fantasma etá po' to' lao"
The ghost was everywhere, he said.
In the air, the palm trees, in his hair.
He could feel it with his soles,
in the movement of the dirt as he stood.
But it was a strange ghost, one he could not see.
He would notice how this apparition would reach
its skeletal fingers silently, skillfully, as fishbones
that turned to steel.
It took hold of him, how in time
each cell in his body could feel
its presence.
     "Vete pa' Nueva Yol," they pleaded.
He did not leave.
It was the white sand, he said, that took root in him.
Then, pointing to a mound near the safety zone,
where the migratory birds were protected, he said,
"My mother is here,"
and she was a ghost he could see.

we swam

IN

Even in the thunder of explosives
there was time for love
In the softness of a woman's long hair
In the arms of lovers
In the glow of a luminescent bay
In the campfires at night
In the building of a chapel

                  In

Cebú Poem: Loggerheads and Leatherbacks

Once in the Caribbean brine,
away from the prying eyes of my father,
lost in blue with the smell of fish-bones on our skin.
I gave myself to you, soft as the inside of a mollusk.

Bashful as the turtles we were chasing.
Coast after coast following the nesting sites,
every egg marked and mapped,
each freckle traced by your finger—naming constellations.

We navigated with the laughter of our crew,
two desperate boys, who robbed at night
the future of those nests, unseen to us 'the protectors'
while we stole each other's breath under the *Antinous* stars.

Plundered nests before the sun entered those waters,
under the fading eye of *Yucayú*,
just as you left without saying *adiós*
leaving me alone on sand, ocean, and new discovered fire.

1970* half life
"Culebra para los culebrenses."

That day in March,
the boats painted in the gaudy
colors of *el Caribe* floated empty
no red flag impeded their passage
the waters were serene,
a leatherback swam to shore,
a Least tern rolled
three eggs in her nest,
and the men found their tongues
in the shell of a mollusk

they stood firm under the sharpshooters
poised on the occupied hill
rifles ready as fishing spears,
—*No tresspassing*
but unlike fish, the men on the other side of the barbwire
were armed
with conchs, the queen conch, *Strombus gigas*
raised in unison
as when they heralded a great catch.
Seventy conchs strong
singing
with the willingness of a hurricane
inside those nautical chambers
air trembled as cathedral glass in the eye
of an incoming tropical storm

The island was a colony

a blue bowl that screamed
autonomy

from predator hands
that tore its center

a mastectomy of bombs
shattering living corals

into floating dead bees
on a fluid ocean

The National Environmental Policy Act
January 1, 1970

Sec. 2 [42 USC § 4321]. The purposes of this Act are: To declare a national policy which will encourage productive and enjoyable harmony between man and his environment; to promote efforts which will prevent or eliminate damage to the environment and biosphere and stimulate the health and welfare of man; to enrich the understanding of the ecological systems and natural resources important to the Nation; and to establish a Council on Environmental Quality.

harmony
      harmony
            harmony
damage
         done
                how long does the radiation
                         lasts?

half life*_____?

Ode to a small turtle
Eretmochelys imbricata

Personal strata are not dated
like fossils on a red flag
there aren't any half-lives
without radiation
only the experience of shared surface
that rumbled and tore

naval practices of Walleye bombs
during a brief geological
moment of time
creating memorial imprints
—a tank deserted on today's tourist beach
—a sign for divers, 'beware not to stand
    explosive mines on sand'

Like a Hawksbill turtle
sitting on the middle of a target
on a cay shorn bald of vegetation
that endangered
endearing
single female
choosing a nest site
to save a community
of fish
birds
coral
and the personal strata
geographical dream
of the people of Culebra

Dedication:

After Hurricane María

Colonizaton makes
the skin stretch too tight.
Witness!

      —tension never strays far.
It lies a hungry dog
under muscle and bone
snapped awake by rustling of flags
and the diction of laws
'posses, redistribute, starve.'
And yet,
there were moments of exquisite gain

1975   —a Molotov cocktail made of a student's
expensive stockings
1968   —a gathering on a beach with a warm breeze
that smelled of Caribe's dreams

and aroma of sea water and courage
different then
like no before, no after.

Mainly we gathered baskets of loss,
    —still gather after so many hurricanes

Even today, after all these years
the memories of our chants and marches,
—our naiveté born in our collective youth seeking a future
of our own, imagining our lives free

the hungry dog no longer starving.

And now, those images that were buried
under the heaviness of sand,
with all the ugly rhetoric,
"the grossly incompetent, nothing there works"
return
awakes the hunger, makes the skin s t r e t c h anew.

Amelia Díaz Ettinger was born in Mexico, but was raised by her paternal family in Puerto Rico. She began writing poetry at age three, dictating poems out loud to the adults in her life who wrote them down for her. During her early teens she would travel by ferry to the small municipality of Culebra, in pursuit of new birds and turtles for her expanding interest in the natural sciences. In her twenties she ran away to Washington State, to pursue a Master's of Science in Biology and to liberate herself from the hermetic hold the island, and her family, had on her. Amelia continued writing poems and short stories throughout her life, while working as a high school Science and Spanish teacher in the small town of La Grande, Oregon.

Amelia Díaz Ettinger poems reflect the struggle with identity often found in immigrants and the confusion of growing up on a colonial island. Oregon poet laureate, Peter Sears, said of her poetry "… *These recollections pulse with energy, and they echo the poetry of Lorca and Neruda.*"

In this chapbook, the author retells in lyric form her recollections of events on the island of Culebra, a municipal island of Puerto Rico. During these visits, in pursuit of birds, and turtles, she found more than the nature of ecology. She found a history of violence and triumph that would leave an indelible mark on her life.

The author is currently pursuing an MFA in Creative Writing at Eastern Oregon University. Her poetry and short stories have appeared in journals, magazines, and anthologies. Presently, she has two collections of poetry. Her first collection was published in 2015 by RedBat Press, *Speaking at a Time*. Her second book *Learning to Love a Western Sky* is available from Airlie Press.

CPSIA information can be obtained
at www.ICGtesting.com
Printed in the USA
BVHW031653070321
601462BV00001B/13